Queen Anne Boleyn

Dedicated to
Lucy Churchill
&
Kathryn Holeman
who have supported me through this work and with whom I share a passion for history & art

Written and illustrated
By
Rebecca Monet

And a Very Special Thanks to...

Natalie Grueninger and all the intriguing guests she interviews on her podcast, "Talking Tudors" at onthetudortrail.com; as well as the numerous historians and writers, such as **Professor Eric Ives OBE, Professor Suzannah Lipscomb** and **Alison Weir** (to name only a few!) who have filled my days with an in-depth understanding of Anne; **Sarah Morris** and **Claire Ridgway** who fascinated me with their virtual YouTube tours and detailed video discussions; historian **Dr. Owen Emmerson** who graciously hosted me, virtually, at **Hever Castle** in Kent where he is clearly a personable and astute supervisor; and **my friends and family** who have always supported my creative efforts—especially **my husband and children** who not only made it possible for me to complete this project, but enjoyed the creation of each page along with me.

And to my dear friend Elizabeth Dishman, I chortle, "The fabrics! The fabrics!"

About the Author

Rebecca Money is a writer and illustrator who grew up in the state of Maryland in the U.S. She received a BFA in illustration, cum laude, from Georgia State University. She successfully created custom murals in private homes in Atlanta, Georgia for nearly twenty years; after which, she has spent the last fifteen years as a mother and writer. Her mural clients used to jokingly call her "Rebecca Monet." It wasn't until her last year of painting murals when her father discovered, through a genealogy-fascinated cousin, her clients were not off the mark. She has since adopted **Rebecca Monet** as her pen name. A perennial student at heart, she loves history, flamenco and going really fast on carting tracks.

"I think Anne would have especially loved the latter and I enjoy the thought of seeing her, French hood flying, as she beats everyone else to the finish line." ~ R.M.

Queen Anne Boleyn: Her intriguing life in historically detailed illustrations and quotations
Copyright © 2020 Rebecca Money Johnson. All Rights Reserved.
Written and Illustrated by Rebecca Monet

All rights reserved. Duplicating pages by scanning and electronic sharing of any parts of this book without permission of the publisher is considered unlawful piracy and theft of the author's intellectual property. If you would like to use material from this book (other than for review purposes or social media photos encouraged by the author), written permission must be obtained by contacting the author at: anneboleynpaperdoll@gmail.com

First Edition: October 2020

ISBN: 978-0-578-75412-3

Printed by Bookmobile / bookmobile.com
Typesetting by Kathryn Holeman / KSHCreative.com

Additional copies of this book may be purchased at: AtelierBisoux.Etsy.com

When it All Started: How I Met Anne Boleyn

Like so many Anne aficionados before me, I was simply living my life when Anne Boleyn entered from the periphery. For me, it began when an elegantly attired Tudor lady appeared on my screen during an effort to distract myself from the sting of daily exercise. Inscribed upon her image were the words, *The Last Days of Anne Boleyn*.

Of course, I knew Anne Boleyn was one of the six wives of Henry VIII. I even knew the schoolyard chant, "Divorced, beheaded, died, divorced, beheaded, survived" and often hurled it, from a safe distance, at every Henry VIII I ever saw at a Renaissance Faire. Yet, I could not put a face or individual history to each woman (which is actually rather appalling).

So it began: In the middle of the documentary, I stopped what I was doing, sat down, and watched the rest of the show, *captivated*. Then, I Googled. I fell into an abyss, and—as anyone who has ever *truly* discovered Anne Boleyn—I became completely engrossed in her story.

What I eventually discovered was both maddening and fascinating. In fact, when I looked up the timeline of Anne Boleyn's life, the primary source did not include the apparently little known of—yet highly formative—years Anne spent away from England on "the continent." Yet, it was there—at both the "Low Countries" and in France—where Anne was "finished," and eventually became not only the vibrant and intelligent young lady-in-waiting who entered Henry VIII's court, but the woman who is still capable of captivating us today.

These events—which made Anne truly extraordinary—are rarely recognized. Instead, they are often replaced by a vacuum; a void which has been precipitously filled with the useful fodder of propagandist writings against Anne because of her religious views. It seems Anne's life has been chiefly reduced to three events: her estimated birth year, her alleged scheme to take Henry VIII away from his wife—and, of course, her execution. For many, this diminished triptych seems to be the sum of Anne.

However, she was far from this caricature. On the contrary, she was so much more. For one, although she was not considered the most beautiful woman at Henry VIII's court, her time abroad and her excellent education certainly must have made her the most intriguing. Consequently, when I try to imagine what she was really like, I think of the women I know who are not conventionally beautiful, but their mind, spirit and elegance combine to form an impervious force—something entirely untouchable and enigmatic.

The French attempt to capture this phenomenon with the phrase *je ne sais quoi (I do not know what)*. However, perhaps it was Shakespeare who best pinned it down when he said of Cleopatra, "Age cannot wither her, nor custom stale / Her infinite variety." In essence, it was most likely Anne's French sensibilities—notably her grace and elegance, which she gleaned from her time abroad—that truly completed Anne, making her highly desirable and undeniably singular.

One of my very good friends is French. She is as intelligent as she is beautiful and graceful—that is to say, she is brilliant. As a professor at an internationally reputed school, she can make picking up a fork look like a work of art. Once we were at a party at her loft, and she was worried about the outcome of something baked—or the lack of silverware, I can't remember which—and a mutual friend of ours said, "No worries. There is not a person here, man or woman, who wouldn't eat off your fingers."

When I think of Anne Boleyn's French influence, I think of that moment at my friend's party and I feel I have some understanding as to why Henry VIII changed the very fiber of his kingdom to make Anne his wife. Though she was not the best looking woman at court, clearly Anne's intellect and—as one of Cardinal Wolsey's servants pointed out—her "excellent grace and behavior" had Henry VIII eating out of her hand.

What followed on the heels of my plunge into Anne's life was perhaps not too unlike Dickens' unprecedented speed while writing "A Christmas Carol" or Handel's fevered strokes composing "The Messiah." Though I do not count myself their equal by any stretch, I did feel a similar frenzied inspiration while researching and creating this paper doll. I loved peeling back the many layers of Anne's story and drawing in the details. I literally wanted to offer a full, well rounded picture of Anne and I did not look up until it was done. I relished every minute of it. I hope these colouring pages transport you, as they did me, into the days of Anne's life nearly 500 years ago, when the newly minted Tudor Dynasty—brandishing its second king—was on the brink . . .

With the exception of the "Hever Rose Portrait," the event pages are in chronological order. Each page has historical details which can be found on the back of the image; along with a complete Bibliography and an Additional Information & Sources by Page in the back of the book. On the fabric of each kirtle/skirt, you will find symbolism imagined from the event on which the drawing was based.

Instructions

Though this is not, in the strictest sense, a "paper doll," it is in fact, a bit more. In the end, your open book will serve as the apparatus for a lovely decorative display. And, with the exception of removing the face area from the dress pages (for the doll's face to peek through), you will keep each page intact.

Step 1: Carefully remove each full page with a craft blade or scissors.

Step 2: Colour the doll page (with Anne in her smock and kirtle).

Step 3: Choose and colour the event/dress page you would like to display, carefully using a craft blade to remove the blank face area. *Note: For some of the pages, you may wish to also remove the area down to the necklace/gown neckline for a more consistent look to the image.* With this, the final display will reveal Anne's face from the doll page underneath.

Step 4: With your doll and chosen dress pages coloured and ready, place your book down on a flat surface and lay your coloured doll page on to the front cover.

Step 5: Overlay your chosen dress page on top until the face of the doll page peeks through. If you wish, you may colour and assemble the optional border edges and lay the completed border on the very top to cover any rough edges, or just to complete the look.

Step 6: Use two decorative paper clips at the top to secure all of the layers onto the front cover of your book. Now, open up the book covers and place them vertically to stand on their own. The result is a beautiful display you may change out whenever you wish.

A rendering of the final display can be seen on the Optional Book Stands & Display Borders page . I chose some elegant tassel paper clips for the final touch. Purchase information is in the back of the book. There are several other beautiful decorative paper clips on Etsy.com or you can create your own!

There are a few options to fortify your display, if necessary. For instance, the provided stands may be useful—or, you may simply place a smaller hardback book inside your standing covers in order to keep them propped up.

You may also opt to put the completed display on your wall, or a bulletin board, or attach everything onto another frame, purchased or made. *Let your creativity reign!* I feel confident Anne would love your unique response…

The face on the doll was inspired by one of the two Holbein sketches traditionally believed to depict Anne Boleyn and checked against *The Moost Happi Portrait Medal* restored by sculptor Lucy Churchill (the Holbein sketch is featured below). However, feel free to reduce and cut out an image of how you see Anne (for instance, Natalie Dormer or Geneviève Bujold?) and attach it to the doll page. We all have our favorites, so have fun!

Of course, "the sky's the limit" on colouring styles, too! You can make the kirtle appear to be a damask by outlining the motifs and/or shading them in darkly, then shade the whole surface of the kirtle very lightly with the same colour (or vice versa). Perhaps consider metallic markers, or applying small costume jewels, or taking a modern approach with both color and style. Additionally, there are some wonderful online tutorials for rendering various textures (fur, velvet, etc). It is your display, so make it your own!

Who is Anne Boleyn? I discovered a very complex, moving woman

~ Lucy Churchill
Sculptor; Creator of the restored
"The Moost Happi" portrait medal;
interview on the "Talking Tudors" podcast, episode #29 with Natalie Grueninger

Foreward

There is an abundance of incarnations of Anne Boleyn both in popular culture and in historical studies of her life. Indeed, rarely are we presented with the same version of Anne. You may have seen her gloved and in sleek black apparel; smouldering on-screen as a scheming and privileged temptress. Perhaps you have also met a prickly puppet with her strings pulled until they snapped by an ambitious but spineless family. Or you may have read of a radical saint on a crusade to rid England of external spiritual and temporal governance. The Annes we are given are almost always flat, with only ever one or two overarching characteristics holding her up for us to judge her by. Rarely do we see a rounded and at times contradictory character. We are invited to be either with or against her. Not so here.

For someone so seemingly recognisable, we barely have an idea what Anne looked like. This innovative and carefully curated book, comprised of up-to-date information and thought about Anne's life, alongside stunning imagery of it, invites us to bring into vivid colour the woman we picture. It allows us to explore the many facets to Anne's character, question the events that shaped it and consider the role that Anne herself played in shaping the profound political and spiritual shifts that enveloped her rise to Queen. By visiting Anne's education in the Low Countries and France, for example, a far more cultured, charitable, and pious woman emerges from the page. Anne wasn't always likeable, but she was always fascinating.

Like all women who were cut down on the scaffold, or accused of the crimes that she was, Anne's character and actions have been tried many times over since her uncle pronounced her guilt before her peers on 15th May 1536. Anne herself knew this would be the case. Amongst her last recorded words four days later was a plea: that if anyone "meddled of" her cause, she required them to "judge the best." I cannot help but feel that she would be 'moost happi' with this thoughtful endeavour.

~ **Dr. Owen Emmerson**, Social and Cultural Historian
Castle Supervisor at Hever Castle, the childhood home of Anne Boleyn in Kent, England

Anne Boleyn Paper Doll

By way of introduction, the statement at the top of this page is Anne's classic phrase, *the time will come*, emboldened further by her name; a phrasing gleaned from one of the signatures in her prayer book which was originally in French ("le temps viendra"). It is shown again, in her own handwriting, on the next image (Anne's *Hever Rose* portrait).

The astrolabe in the right corner—a classic instrument which was used to calculate the movement of the stars and other heavenly bodies like the sun and moon—denotes time. This is an homage to the delightfully small, rudimentary astrolabe Anne also drew by the "time" phrase in her prayer book.

Historian Professor Suzannah Lipscomb's quote points out not only what was most confusing about Anne, but also what was *best* about Anne—that is to say, her astonishing complexity; an elixir of charm and intelligence which still holds our fascination today.

As to Anne's clothes, it may go without saying, a woman's dress in Tudor times had many layers. Both the smock and kirtle, which Anne is wearing in this image, would be slipped on (as well as the decorative, separate inner sleeves) before the gown was laced on top—making this doll the perfect base for the individual dress pages ahead.

The smock Anne is seen wearing has traditional embroidery which was used for both piecing the smock together and decorating the cuffs. According to *The Tudor Tailor*, "The smock was made of white linen, the only washable fabric. The Tudor lady had no other underwear. Her knee length woolen stockings, called hose, were woven, not knitted. Rich ladies wore shoes made of dyed leather, satin or velvet to match their clothes." Furthermore, "The kirtle was worn under the gown so the only part to be seen was the front of the skirt. Often an expensive and beautiful silk was used for this. The bodice and back of the skirt were made of a plainer, cheaper silk in the same colour." The gown was secured with laces in the front.

The fashionably flat silhouette of the bodice was achieved by both an under garment made of stiffened fabric (which Anne is wearing here, over her smock) and by a *placard*. The latter was often the final touch—a piece of flat, fortified fabric (of the same or complimentary fabric to the dress) pinned to the front of the gown to cover the laces.

Enraptured by the spirit of the white falcon, her heraldic symbol, Anne is shown here in a kirtle graced with classic Tudor symbols signifying her queenship as well as small bouquets of Hawthorne or "May flowers" which can also be seen in her hand. The "May flowers" serve as a reminder of her death on 19 May 1536.

Hever Rose Portrait Page

Certainly a treasured favorite, Anne Boleyn's *Hever Rose* portrait at Hever Castle is uniquely immortalized on this page by using varying details from the painting itself. It is no surprise Dr. Owen Emmerson, historian and supervisor at Hever Castle, feels the *Hever Rose* portrait "is a personal favorite."

Regarding the painting's provenance (origins), Emmerson goes on to say "it has a massive question mark over it. It's really rather exciting. It's recognized by most of Anne's biographers and historians as a connection between the likenesses that we know of Anne . . . it wasn't purchased by (the current owners of Hever) the Guthrie family and it wasn't purchased by the Astors, either."

Emmerson also points out there have been many references to the portrait's interminable presence at Hever. In fact, a group of artists visiting Hever in the 1860's refer to it as an "ancient" painting of Anne. Given most of the portraits we have of Anne are not, in fact, contemporary, but created later (mostly during the Elizabethan era), it is very likely the *Hever Rose* portrait could be an exception. "We know no provenance for it. It has no provenance and it is very likely it has been at Hever for a very long time. That in and of itself absolutely fascinates me."

The large roses depicted in the background are the distinctive "Hever Castle Rose". Known for its "velvety deep-red blooms," the "Hever Castle Rose" was "bred by the highly regarded rose hybridizer, the late Colin Horner . . . (it) has a long flowering period from May to the first frost in October . . . (and) after its launch by Dame Judi Dench in 2011, the 'Hever Castle Rose' has settled in well in the grounds and can now be seen gracing (the) renowned walled rose garden (at Hever)."

On this image, heraldic symbols which belonged to both Anne Boleyn's parents have been imagined to adorn Anne's kirtle. The Bull head at the top is, of course, from her father's heraldry. The lion belongs to the Howards, a highly prominent family during the Tudor era and one to which her mother, Elizabeth, belonged. Contrary to popular belief, Anne's family was well placed in English society long before she became a courtier herself.

Inscribed upon this image is "Le temps viendra" ("The time will come") along with a tiny hand-drawn astrolabe. Both are depicted just as they appear, in Anne's own hand, within one of her prayer books. This prayer book and one other are on permanent display at Hever Castle.

Hever Page

In all probability, Anne was born in Norfolk, but as a young child, her father, Thomas, moved the family to Hever Castle in Kent to be closer to the king's court. She spent much of her childhood at Hever and it was most likely a place of refuge for her during the turbulent years of *The Great Matter* (Henry's desire for an annulment from his marriage to Katherine of Aragon).

"The landscape you would see (if you were with Anne at Hever) is the Kentish Weald," notes Hever supervisor and historian Dr. Owen Emmerson, " . . . and what you would overwhelmingly see, is oak. The weald was famous for its vast sways of great oak trees. Because of this high proportion of dense forests, the weald became an incredibly rich place in the Tudor era for the iron industry; the wood being used as charcoal to power the furnaces."

Emmerson also points out you would have seen a number of buildings committed to farming activities for what was largely a self-sustaining community in service to the castle. Today, Hever boasts of lovely Italianate gardens and a charming Tudor village behind the castle, all created by its previous owner, William Waldorf Astor, in the early 20th century.

Consequently, this page depicts Anne standing before the base of an oak tree, wearing the traditional 16th century English gabled hood, which she may have worn as a young girl at Hever. Noted for her love of learning, she is seen holding a book in her hand. Her skirt is imagined with the flora and fauna you may see at the gardens at Hever today. The image of Hever is drawn with its modern additions to honor the memory of those who have visited the grounds in recent times.

Mechelen

Contrary to popular belief, Anne's father, Sir Thomas Boleyn, was already a successful courtier and well established long before his daughters became a part of Henry VIII's court. Most notably, he was a successful ambassador to Mechelen, in the highly influential Low Countries, on Henry's behalf. As such, he was well liked by the regent, Margaret of Austria, and openly welcomed to her court at Mechelen. Sir Thomas, seeing an opportunity, asked Margaret if Anne could enter service to her. Margaret's appreciation for Thomas' good humor and diplomatic skills was assured when Margaret indeed summoned the young Anne to court to fill one of only a few sought-after positions as one of her maids of honor.

Mechelen's influence cannot be overstated. The center of culture and a true Renaissance court, Mechelen boasted the comings and goings of artists, statesmen and many thinkers of the age—including cutting-edge religious reformers and respected humanists such as Erasmus; not to mention the influence of Margaret herself, a woman who would lead diligently and wisely over many men and many complicated situations. In the words of the late historian Professor Eric Ives, "Anne Boleyn could have no better mentor." This had an enormous impact on the young Anne, and truly wove into her being—and psyche—the progressive thinking and graces she would later exhibit at the English court.

This page shows Anne in Renaissance-inspired attire, strolling to her French lesson with her tutor, Monsieur Symmonet, along the arched walkway bordering the inner courtyard at Mechelen. The walls are graced with the "English bond:" brickwork which is made up of alternating courses of stretchers and headers. This enormously strong construct forms a series of interlocking crosses, causing the mortar to proliferate the illusion of lovely concentric diamonds along the surface of the walls.

Anne's skirt exhibits one of Margaret's symbols—a pelican stabbing at a heart—which denotes charity, an attribute exhibited in Margaret's own life. More specifically, it reflects Margaret's deep concern for the welfare and education of children. Later at Henry's court, Anne would take issue with the use of the dissolved monasteries. Instead of being reserved for schools or charity (as she had hoped), Thomas Cromwell, chief minister to Henry VIII, often sold them to nobles for the king's profit.

Chateau de Blois

The influences of the court in France, where Anne was sent after her short time with Margaret of Austria, were no less than transformative. Originally called up from Mechelen due to her French language skills, Anne was to serve Mary Tudor in France upon Mary's marriage to Louis XII. When Louis XII died only a few months later, Anne remained in order to serve his daughter Queen Claude, who now reigned over France with her husband, Francis I. Quiet, demure and concerned for the things of God as well as current Italian fashions, Claude was a woman of elegance, gentleness and piety.

Consequently, if we think of the French Court of the early 16th century, it is best to invite images of the Italian Renaissance—not Louis XIV's court over a hundred years later—and Leonardo was a key player. For one, it is most likely Leonardo's influence behind the famous circular steps at Francis I's Chateau de Blois (seen to the left side of this image) and he would have walked along the same halls as Anne. It is sheer speculation if they met, but it seems to me, as part of the same court, and as part of the many cultural events in which Anne would have sometimes taken part (and which most likely Leonardo would have been responsible for designing and planning), it is not too far-fetched to think they may have passed one another at least once, as denoted here, in this drawing.

"It may well be hard to imagine Leonardo within the same period as King Henry VII and his son (Henry VIII) . . . something may seem to jar a little with these thoughts with us at first; however, Leonardo was indeed a part of the Tudor period, painting his way through the cities of Milan, Florence, Rome and Paris, to name but a few." These words from Amanda Harvey Purse, author and Tudor historian, sum up exactly how we may feel when we see Leonardo da Vinci standing beside Anne and playing a part in Anne's story. However, both Anne and Leonardo were very much a part of the court of Francis I. As noted on the site chambord.org: "Following the Battle of Marignano, François I discovered the marvels of Italian architecture and, more specifically, the work of Leonardo da Vinci. When he returned to France (in 1516), he invited the polymath genius to sojourn in the French court as 'premier painter, architect and engineer of the king.'" Clearly Leonardo was a central figure in Francis I's court, and Anne very likely enjoyed his influences.

During her years on the continent—nearly a decade—Anne learned, among many things, to sing, dance and play the lute; and she was privy to the minds and works of some of the greatest artists and thinkers of the age. This certainly informed the stunning, bright star who emerged upon Henry VIII's court in 1522.

In this drawing, Anne's kirtle holds the symbols of Francis I's court with the fleurs-de-lis embedded shield and the crowned salamander; the latter proliferating a nearly phoenix-like legend in that it was said to be able to withstand fire for the sake of virtue. Francis I's motto was "I nourish and I extinguish." Although not drawn here, the symbols specific to Queen Claude were the pierced swan and the crowned ermine, often seen in friezes at Chateau de Blois. The prolific crowned porcupine belonged to Louis XII.

Masque

After her years on the European continent, it seems uniformly agreed upon Anne's first recorded appearance at the court of Henry VIII was the *Chateau Vert* masque at York Place on Shrovetide, 4 March 1522.

The masque, as a genre, was a form of courtly entertainment and could be defined as a "lyrical drama" with its roots firmly planted in the Italian Renaissance. This is key when it comes to Anne. Again, in the early sixteenth century, the royal courts of Europe adopted their cultural cues from the Italian Renaissance. Tudor England was, if you will pardon the pun, a little late to the ball. Anne had experienced masques at both Mechelen and the court of Francis I, where they had been a part of court entertainment for much longer than they had been enjoyed by English courtiers. For this reason, the masques she experienced on the continent were likely more deeply cultivated. As Natalia Richards, author of "The Falcon's Flight," has stated, this fact made Anne more "ahead of the game" when she took part in the *Chateau Vert* masque. This knowledge and sophistication made her stand out among the other female courtiers.

The visual narrative of the *Chateau Vert* (also known as *The Assault on the Castle Virtue* masque), as described by Holly Dugan (author of "The Ephemeral History of Perfume"), is taken from Edward Hall's account:

"The sumptuous costumes and special effects of the masque celebrated sensual pleasure. Anne, cast as Perseverance, defended the titular castle of virtue along with seven other ladies, each dressed in a Milanese gown of white satin, wearing bonnets of gold, embroidered with their allegorical part: Beauty, Honor, Kindness, Bounty, Constance, Mercy, and Pity. Banners of hearts, rent or given freely, flew on each tower. Below in the Battlements . . . the female personas of Danger, Distain, Unkindness, Scorn, Malbouche (slander), and Strangeness lay in wait. The lords besieged the castle with oranges, dates, and 'other fruits of pleasure' while the ladies defended themselves with rosewater."

In short, through the narrative and props of the Chateau Vert masque, Henry VIII was showing off his virility, as well as his prominence politically and economically, in order to impress upon the Imperial ambassador his potency as a monarch.

The one thing blatantly missing for Henry was a male heir. Interestingly, Anne entered the Tudor court at such a time when Henry's power was being defined more acutely and the need for a male heir strongly pronounced.

On this page, Anne's kirtle has been imagined displaying highly stylized dates (real dates grow in fuller bunches) and oranges; the exotic fruits used by Henry and fellow male courtiers as "ammunition" to free the virtues from the castle.

The rendering of Anne's "Milan Bonnet" is the result of extensive research—mainly from paintings of Queen Anne of Hungary and numerous other contemporary portraits, as well as Edward Hall's descriptions. I chose to put the word "Perseverance" on her dress, though in actuality, it may have been on her hat.

Courtship

The Courtship of Anne and Henry was long (nearly eight years) and fraught with more interpretations than I care to delineate. However, I will venture to explain the renderings on this page through my own researched lens.

I tend to follow the line of historian Professor Suzannah Lipscomb and many others—that is to say, Anne and Henry were truly in love—and this is logically concluded. As a layperson to history, I agree the facts leading to their courtship certainly befit a perfect storm. The tempest begins with Henry's royal duties (the need for a male heir), not his seduction. Henry's father had begun the Tudor Dynasty and Henry did not presume to end it.

While Henry felt a growing uncertainty towards his marriage due to the need for a male heir, Anne Boleyn—young, graceful, witty and accomplished—an outlier—had been establishing her reputation at court. In time, she had effortlessly distinguished herself among the other young women in service to the queen. After all, Henry could have chosen anyone for a "quick fix." However, he not only chose Anne but waited nearly eight years to make her his legitimate wife. In the process, he changed the very fabric of his kingdom to have her.

Clearly, he had grown to value and respect her—far more than when he first desired her and had basically asked her to be his "Maîtresseen-titre" (Chief Royal Mistress), which she refused. Also, it would be a good four years after Anne's arrival to court before Henry's attraction could even be evidenced. In a love letter to her, dating some time after May 1527, he pleaded to know her feelings "having been above a whole year stricken with the dart of love." This puts his romantic interest beginning in late 1525/early 1526. From that point on, he began to seriously pursue this unique woman who, as Professor Lipscomb states, was enticingly "cosmopolitan", "pious" and "complex."

Consequently, Anne's skirt depicts designs from a very small gold whistle which was the type of object Henry would have attached to his garment to give away as a sort of "party favor" at a pageant or masque and it was one of his very first gifts to Anne. "Above all, it tells a message…" Professor Lipscomb notes, "…and the message is clear. Henry is saying, 'If you whistle, I will come.'" This special attention is highly revelatory regarding Henry's feelings for Anne.

The ship pendant in the upper left-hand corner depicts a gift Anne gave Henry for reasons which vary according to different historians. But for the most part, it can be agreed upon that in the summer of 1527, Anne is most likely saying to Henry, "I give myself into your hands." The design is inspired by the pendant shown on the series "The Tudors." The pendant Anne gave Henry was rich in symbolism, a prominent concept in Tudor jewelry. Drawing on the research of the late Professor Eric Ives, Sarah Morris from "The Tudor Tour Guide," points out: The ship, like the ark in the Bible, carries the idea of protection, something which Anne is asking of Henry; and the diamond dangling from the bottom represents enduring love.

This page also contains Anne's prayer book which Henry and Anne used to basically "pass notes in class"— inscribing messages thick with meaning under carefully chosen images—which they both wrote and read, possibly while in chapel. The message "By daily proof you shall me find, to be to you both loving and kind" was inscribed by Anne under the annunciation of Christ to Mary by the angel Gabriel—a clear message to Henry saying, "I will give you a son". Henry also wrote a message, but under the suffering Christ, as if to say he too suffers, but for Anne's love. He wrote in French: "If you remember my love in your prayers as strongly as I adore you, I shall hardly be forgotten, for I am yours. Henry R. forever."

The Moost Happi

This page delineates the life-changing events behind Anne's motto, "The Moost Happi," when Henry and Anne finally cemented their relationship in late 1532 and early 1533. As Lucy Churchill, who studiously and artfully restored the *Moost Happi Portrait Medal*, states, "moost happi" in Tudor times actually meant "moost lucky" and it seems around this time, things were certainly going Anne's way . . .

Henry, having made Anne the "Marquis of Pembroke," took her with him to Calais in late 1532 in order for her to gain both recognition and approval from Francis I—a gesture which Henry hoped would bolster his request for Francis I to present his desire for a marriage annulment before the Pope.

The consummation of their union, which led to Anne's first pregnancy, is considered the result of either a betrothal or perhaps, according to chronicler Edward Hall, a secret marriage; which took place on their return to Dover from Calais on 14 November 1532 (St Erkenwald's Day). Either way, notes Natalie Grueninger (on her website onthetudortrail.com), Anne and Henry clearly began to co-habitate as they most likely conceived around early December, 1532—assuming their baby, the future Elizabeth I, was born in good time (7 September 1533).

Then, on the 25th of January, 1533, at the chapel within the Holbein Gate at Whitehall Palace (with Anne already nearly two months pregnant), they were married in a secret ceremony. That is, either they married again, more "officially," or for the first time.

As Grueninger again points out, with this long-awaited union, Anne's impending coronation, and what they felt would be the birth of their "son," Anne adopted the motto "The Moost Happi." However, the *Moost Happi Portrait Medal* itself, which is shown in the upper right-hand corner, was crafted during her second pregnancy in 1534—a pregnancy which was originally noted by the Imperial ambassador's written observation of Anne's "goodly belly" but most likely ended in a miscarriage or stillbirth. In the end, it is not clear as to why this pregnancy—along with the production of the medal—abruptly ended.

The Moost Happi Portrait Medal, however, is a precious artifact. It is the only existing image we can confirm, with complete certainty, to be made during Anne's lifetime. Sculptor Lucy Churchill noted "the details of her costume are so precisely depicted in the medal (despite its tiny size) that it's possible to recognise the exact same Gable Hood and jewelry in Holbein's 1536 portrait of Jane Seymour. Given that her costume has been so carefully reproduced, it stands to reason that Anne's features would have been equally well observed and skillfully rendered....Knowing how conscious and controlling she was about her appearance, I think this medal represents how Anne wanted to be seen."

On this page, Anne's dress reflects a gown from the film "Anne of the Thousand Days." Her kirtle takes inspiration from the iconography in the Rood Screen at Kings College Chapel in Cambridge. More specifically, it shows one of the most delightful parts of the screen, the HA cipher. In the time of the Tudors, hidden messages in symbols were quite common. Churchill recounts the analysis of the carved HA given by Ives as she points out, "The A —with the stroke through the apex and the normal horizontal written as a V—creates the letters T and M out of the single letter A. By doing that you get the Latin word "amat" (he/she loves)—so the cipher means Henry loves Anne, or Anne loves Henry. Henry and Anne loved these word plays, and this is a beautiful example of it."

Coronation

By 1 June 1533, the fruition of Anne and Henry's dreams can be seen not only in Anne's pregnancy of six months, but in her coronation as Queen of England. One thing is clear from the speed and the sophistication by which the plans were made, Henry did not want her legitimacy—or the legitimacy of their coming child— to be in any way questioned. What is most remarkable, states James Peacock, founder of *The Anne Boleyn Society*, is "Anne was crowned and anointed as a monarch—not just a queen consort." After Anne, Henry did not crown any of his other wives. In fact, Anne Boleyn's coronation would be the last individual coronation of a queen *consort* in English history.

Anne's ermine trimmed robe was said to be of a deep purple, perhaps a color more warm in tone than cool and similar to a deep maroon. Her crown is taken from both Holbein's "doodle" of the seating plan for the coronation feast and research on "St Edward's crown" (of which it is said Anne's crown was commissioned to resemble).

The poem, "Falcon White" was written by Nicolas Udall to honor Anne at her coronation. Udall's support for Anne's religious reforms were further evidenced by the other decorative choices he made for her coronation. Historian Professor Eric Ives confirms there are overt messages in the poem regarding these reforms stating, "What, however, is without a doubt is that the final verses refer to the papal obstructiveness and spell out that justice had at last been done and the country could now relax: 'And where by wrong/She hath flown long/Uncertain where to light/Herself repose/Upon the Rose/Now many this Falcon White/Whereon to rest/And build her nest/GOD grant her, most of might!/That England may rejoice as always/In this same Falcon White.'"

Anne was said to hold a scepter and a rod, but as a matter of design, I have chosen the orb along with the scepter. On this scepter is the head of a white falcon, her heraldic symbol. I chose white falcons to grace her kirtle as a white falcon reigns over what was her official badge, designed at the time of her coronation (as seen to the right of the image).

Tower

If it is not enough, the indictment against Anne is largely erroneous (accusing her of being in places she never was, in liaisons she was unlikely to have committed while dealing with pregnancies which ended in a birth and miscarriage), then perhaps Anne's final confession of innocence—a confession from a pious queen in a religious age— should be considered in her favor? If not, certainly the speed of her imprisonment, trial and death should indicate something was amiss? That is, if the whole of this evidence does not give pause? As it was, most prisoners spent months and sometimes over a year—or even numerous years— in the tower before their end. Anne's arrest, trial and death took a little less than three weeks. Her fall was dramatic and bewildering, even to her enemies.

Eustace Chapuys, the Imperial ambassador and one of Anne's greatest detractors (and one of Katherine of Aragon's greatest supporters), felt pity on her as "Anne was, in Chapuys' eyes, an innocent woman. His words (at the time of her death) are heartfelt in their admiration:

'No one ever shewed more courage or greater readiness to meet death than she did, having, as the report goes, begged and solicited those under whose keeping she was to hasten the execution. When orders came from the King to have it [the execution] delayed until today, she seemed sorry, and begged and entreated the governor of the Tower for God's sake, to go to the King, and beg of him that, since she was well disposed and prepared for death, she should be dispatched immediately.'

This final page is intended as a memorial to one of England's most remarkable queens. It is an homage to the moniker purportedly given to Anne by Archbishop Thomas Cranmer when he said, "She who has been the Queen of England on earth will today become a Queen in Heaven."

Rather than recount her time on the scaffold, I have created a montage of remembrance beginning with the large basket of roses in the background; a reference to the roses anonymously left every year on 19 May on her memorial tile at the Tower of London. The shield featured on her memorial tile is depicted on the upper right-hand corner of the page and the design on the damask fabric of her ermine cloak mimics the circular vines around the edge of the tile. Her hair, dress and crown were inspired by Joan Bergin's designs worn in "The Tudors" series—in appreciation of their elegance, which I believe, serve to remind us this was a true Queen of England.

I leave you with an echo from the scaffold on May 19, 1536:

Meddle well. Judge best…

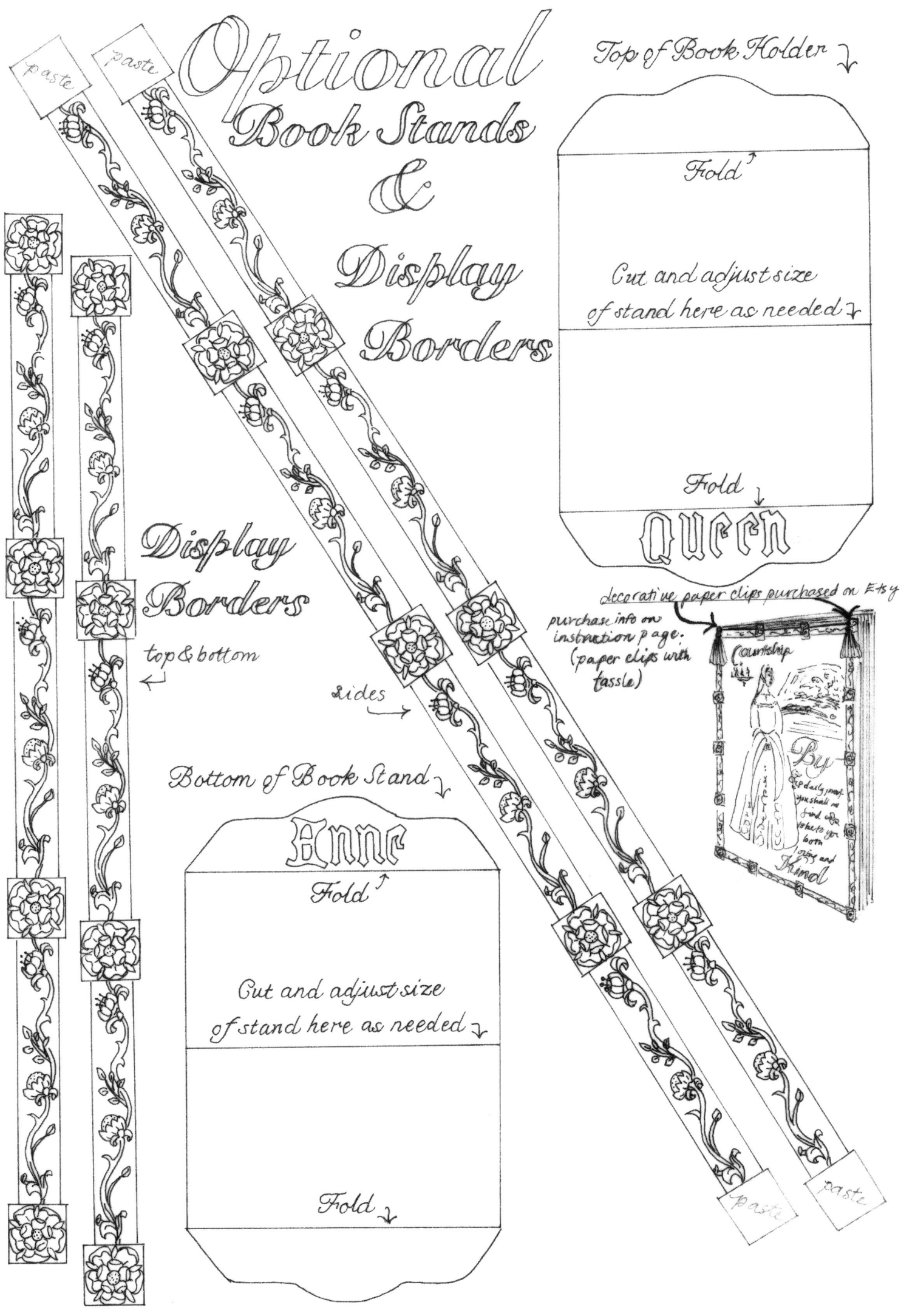

Books which have Informed the Pages of this Colouring Book:

Bordo, Susan. *The Creation of Anne Boleyn: In Search of the Tudors' Most Notorious Queen*. Oneworld, 2014.

Dugan, Holly. *The Ephemeral History of Perfume: Scent and Sense in Early Modern England*. Johns Hopkins University Press, 2011.

Emmerson & Ridgway. *Hever: A Castle and its People*. (date and publisher TBD as of publication)

Ives, Eric. *The Life and Death of Anne Boleyn: The Most Happy*. Blackwell, 2009.

Lipscomb, Suzannah. *1536: The Year that Changed Henry VIII*. Lion Books, 2012.

Mackay, Lauren. *Inside the Tudor Court: Henry VIII and his Six Wives through the eyes of the Spanish Ambassador*. Amberley, 2015.

Morris, Sarah. *Le Temps Viendra*. Spartan Publishing, 2013.

Morris & Grueninger. *In the footsteps of Anne Boleyn*. Amberley, 2015.

Richards, Natalia. *The Falcon's Rise: A Novel of Anne Boleyn*. MADEGLOBAL Pub., 2019.

Vasoli, Sandra. *Struck with the Dart of Love*. MADEGLOBAL Pub., 2016.

Vasoli, Sandra. *Truth Endures*. MADEGLOBAL Pub., 2016.

Vasoli, Sandra. *Anne Boleyn's letter from the Tower: A New Assessment*. MADEGLOBAL Pub., 2015.

Weir, Alison. *The lady in the tower: the fall of Anne Boleyn*. Emblem, 2011.

Weir, Alison. *Anne Boleyn, A King's Obsession: A Novel (Six Tudor Queens)*. Ballantine Books, 2017.

Additional Information & Sources by Page:

Etsy shop link to purchase additional copies of the "Queen Anne Boleyn Paper Doll Colouring Book": https://www.etsy.com/shop/AtelierBisoux

Elizabeth—I love your innovative dance and I feel Anne would have loved it, too! Grateful for our friendship all these years!
Dishman & Co. Choreography, New York. DishmanAndCo.org

Introduction:

The Last Days of Anne Boleyn. Directed by Rob Coldstream, performance by Daniel Flynn & Tara Breathnach. BBC, 2013.

On Henry's six wives: As James Peacock, founder of *The Anne Boleyn Society* has said, of all of Henry's wives, "I feel that a lot of times people feel they have to choose a favorite. My favorite is Anne Boleyn—I do feel most drawn to her story—but that doesn't mean to say that I have any less admiration for the other wives…each has their own story—they aren't just connected to Henry—they are also their own figures (of history) as well."

Grueninger, Natalie and James Peacock. *Boleyn Treasures with James Peacock, Episode 80*, Talking Tudors podcast, 27 June 2020. http://onthetudortrail.com/Blog/2020/06/27/episode-80-boleyn-treasures-with-james-peacock/

Note: During this time period, *The Low Countries* consisted of present day Belgium, Netherlands, and Luxembourg as well as parts of northern France and western Germany.

Cardinal Wolsey was the Archbishop of England who essentially controlled all matters of state for Henry VIII beginning around 1514. In addition to being a cardinal in the Catholic Church, he held several other important roles in England such as *Papal Legate*—an extremely high post. He was essentially the Pope's representative in England and empowered to tend to important ecclesiastical matters. Hence, the *Legatine Court* which Wolsey oversaw in the hopes to extract Henry from his marriage. (Wikipedia, The Anne Boleyn Files)

Instructions:

Lovely tassel paper clips are available from Queso Blanco Designs on etsy.com. Link: https://www.etsy.com/listing/797885217/hand-tied-tassel-paper-clips-bookmarks?ref=shop_home_feat_4

Anne Boleyn Paper Doll:

Note: The Tudor smock is sometimes referred to by using the French term, "chemise."

Henry & Anne: The Lovers Who Changed History. Directed by Chris Mitchell, performance by Professor Suzannah Lipscomb (self), Jack Hawkins & Emma Connell. Lion Television, 2014.

Some of many wonderful resources for the history of Tudor clothing:
~ The Tudor Tailor website: tudortailor.com (also on etsy.com)
~ A Damsel in this Dress website: https://adamselindisdress.blog/tag/16th-century-kirtle/
~YouTube: *Dressing up: A Tudor (Henrician) Lady* by Prior Attire (sponsored by the "Damsel in this Dress" historical seamstress)
~ National Clothing dot org: http://nationalclothing.org/europe/68-england/482-tudor-era-dress-charming-french-gown-of-anne-boleyn-style.html
~ The Anne Boleyn Files: https://www.theanneboleynfiles.com/resources/tudor-life/tudor-clothes/

"What did Anne Boleyn Look Like?" Claire Ridgeway vlog post: https://www.youtube.com/watch?v=RQT9Y8vWPuA

Hever Rose Portrait:

Additional Information:

In this image, a long chained "girdle" hangs from Anne's waist. *The Tudor Tailor* describes this piece of clothing as "tied around the waist for decoration; some were gold and pearl necklaces, but most were made for black silk ribbon and a jewel or tassel at the end."

The Tudor Tailor also describes the construction of Anne's classic "French Hood" as follows: "The very fashionable 'French hood' was a rounded frame, made of wire and stiffened fabric, and covered with silk. Often there were gold beads or even jewels along the edge of this. Around the front edge there was a pleated frill of gold fabric. A black silk veil hung down behind to cover the hair." *The Tudor Tailor* offers many patterns, even one for the French Hood.

Grueninger, Natalie and Dr. Owen Emmerson. *All things Boleyn with Dr. Owen Emmerson, Episode 73*, Talking Tudors podcast, 15 May 2020, http://onthetudortrail.com/Blog/2020/05/15/episode-73-all-things-boleyn-with-dr-owen-emmerson/

Hever Castle Rose information:

https://www.hevercastle.co.uk/news/enjoy-the-beautiful-hever-castle-rose/
tudortailor.com

Hever Page:

Cranmer quote: http://www.luminarium.org/renlit/cranmerhenrymay1536.htm

Weald definition: A heavily wooded area; wild and uncultivated (Merriam-Webster Dictionary)

Grueninger, Natalie and Dr. Owen Emmerson. *All Things Boleyn with Dr. Owen Emmerson, Episode 73*, Talking Tudors podcast, 15 May 2020, http://onthetudortrail.com/Blog/2020/05/15/episode-73-all-things-boleyn-with-dr-owen-emmerson/

Mechelen:

Based on conjecture (from the handwriting in a letter to her father dated 1513), Anne Boleyn was probably born around 1501 and was most likely about 12 years old when she went to Mechelen.

Note: During this time period, The Low Countries consisted of present day Belgium, Netherlands, and Luxembourg as well as parts of northern France and western Germany.

Grueninger, Natalie and Natalia Richards. *All Things Boleyn with Natalia Richards, Episode 72*, Talking Tudors podcast, 8 May 2020. http://onthetudortrail.com/Blog/2020/05/08/episode-72-all-things-boleyn-with-natalia-richards/

More on Mechelen from Natalie's website: https://onthetudortrail.com/Blog/anne-boleyn-places/palaces-and-houses/palace-of-mechelen/

Research for the authentication of the distinctive brick bond at Mechelen led to a discussion with Rodney Mims Cook, President of the National Monuments Foundation in the United States, and founder of the Millennium Gate Museum in Atlanta, Georgia. Mr. Cook verified that despite its location, Mechelen absolutely displays the characteristic brickwork of the English bond versus the Flemish bond.

The reason for this was confirmed in an interview with Harry van Royen—the Heritage Coordinator for the Town Council in Niel, Belgium—who concluded, "Mechelen had a strong historical link to England, especially when Margaret of York, the wife/widow of Burgundian duke Charles the Bold, chose to reside in Mechelen from 1477 onwards. A real English court life was established and she also played a minor but important role in the *War of the Roses*…So, a building in English bond must have been a good sight for her to feel more at home. And for English visitors, it is a clear sign that they have arrived at the right building."

Note: When Margaret of York, sister of Richard III and Edward IV, married Charles the Bold in 1468, she became the stepmother to his daughter, Mary of Burgundy. So affectionate was Mary toward her stepmother, she named her own daughter after her: *Margaret of Austria*. Charles died in 1477 and as mentioned above, Margaret of York remained at Mechelen until her death in 1503.

In his blog, *The Curious Traveller*, Eugene Costello points out: "Lovers of art and architecture should not miss the *Hof van Savoye* (the Court of Savoy), also known as *Paleis van Margareta van Oostenrijk*, or the **Palace of Margaret of Austria**. This fabulous—and fabulously preserved—early example of the Renaissance that would sweep Europe is actually one of the first such in northern Europe…a name familiar to English readers lived here for a time: Anne Boleyn…**It was also the inspiration and model for the Palace of Whitehall in London**, grander and greater in its day than the Vatican and Versailles. Sadly, that was destroyed by fire in 1698… so this gem in Mechelen gives modern-day curious travellers a glimpse of what it must have been like…" http://thecurioustraveller.co.uk/three-mechelen-stars-for-flanders-2/

The basic dress lines in this drawing were inspired by two paintings by Leonardo DaVinci: *Lady with an Ermine* and *La belle ferronnière*; as well as the design by Joan Bergin for Natalie Dormer's dress in Season 1, Episode 3 of *The Tudors* series.

Chateau de Blois:

Based on conjecture, Anne Boleyn was probably about 13 or 14 years old when she became part of Queen Claude's court, and around age 21 when she left to go back to England.

For more information on Chateau de Blois architecture: https://www.chambord.org/en/history/the-chateau/architecture/

Grueninger, Natalie and Natalia Richards. *All Things Boleyn with Natalia Richards, Episode 72*, Talking Tudors podcast, 8 May 2020. http://onthetudortrail.com/Blog/2020/05/08/episode-72-all-things-boleyn-with-natalia-richards/

Link to article discussing Leonardo & Anne:

Amanda Harvey Purse, Tudor historian and author of *The Boleyns: From the Tudors to the Windsors*, featured on the Anne Boleyn Files: https://www.theanneboleynfiles.com/leonardo-da-vincis-boleyn/

References for emblems discussed on this page:

https://hemmahoshilde.wordpress.com/2015/05/28/queen-claude-of-france-emblems/

https://hemmahoshilde.wordpress.com/2015/05/21/francis-i-with-his-salamander/

Basic dress lines & hat inspired by Joan Bergin's design for Natalie Dormer in Season 1, Episode 8 of *The Tudors* series.

Masque:

Based on conjecture, Anne Boleyn was about 21 or close to 22 years old when she entered Henry VIII's court.

Edward Hall (c.1496 – c.May 1547) was an English lawyer and historian, best known for his *The Union of the Two Noble and Illustre Families of Lancastre and Yorke*—commonly known as **Hall's Chronicle**—first published in 1548. It was composed of his writings on contemporary events. He was also several times a member of the Parliament of England. (Wikipedia)

Henry VIII "Defender of the Faith" title, digitized manuscript: https://blogs.bl.uk/digitisedmanuscripts/2020/07/defender-of-the-faith.html

masque definition: "A brief lyrical drama (which) heralded the appearance of masquers who descended their pageant to perform figured dances (and) reveled with guests…the theme of the drama…was usually mythological, allegorical or symbolic and was designed to be complimentary to the noble or royal host of the social gathering". The concept of the masque began in Renaissance Italy, where its first incarnation, the "intermezzo," was created under the patronage of Lorenzo de Medici. "During the 16th century, the European continental masque traveled to Tudor England, where it became a court entertainment played before the king. Gorgeous costumes, spectacular scenery with elaborate machinery to move it on and off stage, and rich allegorical verse marked the English masque". (Encyclopedia Britannica)

Additional Information:

The history of *the Chateau Vert* masque, itself, is fascinating, and it explains the image on this page in further detail:

In her book, *The Ephemeral History of Perfume: Scent and Sense in Early Modern England*, the author, Holly Dugan, points to Edward Hall's account in which we learn 1522 was not only a time when Henry had already been conferred with the title "Defender of the Christian Faith" by the Pope (in 1521), but a year marked by pestilence and death and impending war with France. It is important to remember the Pope, along with the Holy Roman Emperor were, in essence, the authority over European monarchs. Consequently, this title, which elevated Henry, was most likely politically motivated and devised to keep Henry loyal to the church—a clear and decisive pushback against the growing movement for religious reform.

Masque (continued):

Hall, as Dugan theorizes, feels there is an irony in the masque narrative which willingly extracts its eroticism from the Pope's unwitting terms regarding Henry's "pulchritude" (beautiful form) as a "pleasure" which "God wrought". These ideas, combined with the fact the masque was planned as a spectacle to impress the visiting Imperial ambassador (the ambassador to the Holy Roman Emperor, Charles V) meant the masque would be laden with political metaphor which would attempt to point to Henry VIII as the most blessed, if not the most potent and powerful monarch in Europe.

With this "multi-sensorial exoticism" (the exotic fruit, fabrics, etc), Dugan intriguingly suggests the following:

"The symbolism of war becomes a tool of erotic play…flying dates and oranges, an expensive and rare gustatory treat, bomb the castle. Retaliating with fruit confit, the virtues mount their defense. Rosewater, a substitute for hot oil, defends the castle, drenching the…women below…(these) exotic details were a part of its eroticism, they were also a key part of its political meaning. The rosewater used to defend the castle, the fruity projectiles, and the silks and dyes that attire its players attest to the scope of foreign commodities within English culture. The irony is profound; Henry solidified his role as defender of the faith by staging his virility with exotic luxury goods. By the end of the decade, one of these luxury goods in particular would help him redefine his kingly power, embodying a different kind of 'pulchritude': rose perfumes."

The Holy Roman Emperor: "Considered *primus inter pares* (first among equals) among other Roman Catholic monarchs across Europe." (Wikipedia)

Link to original songs which may be from the Chateau Vert masque:
https://tudorwritingcircle.com/2018/11/16/oh-drama-tudor-court-revels-and-mary-boleyn-by-christine-plough-article-not-done/

Further description of the Chateau Vert masque from Hall's Chronicle:
https://www.theanneboleynfiles.com/the-early-life-of-anne-boleyn-part-six-the-chateau-vert-pageant/

Courtship:

Additional Information:

The scenario of Henry and Anne's courtship demands we step back and realize Henry was in need of a wife—a new lifelong companion—not a temporary solution. We should not look at the courtship through the scope of what we now know (e.g. Henry's last four marriages in the span of a short decade following Anne's execution). This quick and unfruitful parsing of relationships was not, I am quite sure, "in the plan" when Henry began to seriously court Anne.

In the end, it is up for debate the degree to which Henry felt convicted by the Biblical passage in the book of Leviticus stating marrying his brother's wife would render him childless (meaning—to a sixteenth century monarch—no sons). Henry had married his brother Arthur's wife, Katherine of Aragon. Arthur had passed away shortly after his marriage to Katherine. Most likely weighing in evenly on the scales of conviction and convenience, Henry had hoped the verse in Leviticus would prove useful in getting an annulment from the Pope, thus detaching him from his nearly twenty-year marriage.

Dealing with the despondency of his loyal, yet aging, first wife's inability to provide more children after years of miscarriages (and the death of one baby boy at seven weeks), Henry was in need of a male heir. Their daughter, Mary, was possibly less than ideal—not because of her abilities, but because her eventual marriage to a foreign prince could dilute England's sovereignty.

Henry needed a legitimate male heir—preferably an "heir and a spare"—which meant he needed a legitimate wife. These "royal duties" of Henry's, in my mind, remove the "homewrecker" status from Anne. Also, as historian Professor Lipscomb has pointed out, in an age before contraceptives, it is important to remember Sixteenth century women didn't give themselves up as easily as modern television or movies would like for us to think. There was too much at risk in the form of disease or pregnancy.

It is best to look at the circumstances of the relationship between Henry and Anne through the lens of a sixteenth—not a twenty-first—century mind and perhaps, a royal dynastic one, as well. And anyone who is interested in Anne's story, is not necessarily in support of adultery, but rather hopes to illuminate the entire scenario honestly.

Anne Boleyn had great potential in Henry's mind. In addition to her amiability and accomplishments in courtly entertainments, she was also an intelligent woman who had gleaned an enormous understanding from some of the greatest minds of the age. As such, she not only had the potential to be his wife and the mother of his male heir, but she could offer Henry something even more singular: the new ideas toward religion—which, in turn, endorsed autonomous leadership free from the Pope. In the end, these new ideas would not only completely change the face of England but unwittingly render Henry's rule more imperial if not more ruthless and self-determined going forward. Unfortunately, the very capacity for power Anne helped Henry achieve was eventually turned against her when she was unable to give Henry the ultimate and final assurance: the male heir who would secure the Tudor Dynasty.

The destruction of Anne's letters at the time of her death might lead us to assume Henry was more desperately in love with her than she was with him. As historian Professor Lipscomb concludes, "I think because we don't have her responses, a lot has been written to fill that gap and there's been an assumption that somehow (Anne) was playing hard to get and manipulating Henry. But in practice, I think ultimately, both of them wanted to do what was right…I don't think we should read into the absence of letters from Anne some sense that she was the one holding all the cards." This is one of the most important things to remember when trying to discover the real relationship between Henry and Anne.

By not only reading Henry's letters firsthand at the Vatican, but also observing *how* he wrote them—which has led to some of her theories on the emotions of *both* Anne and Henry—Sandra Vasoli (currently an author of three books about Anne Boleyn and her relationship with Henry) had some very insightful things to say in her interview with Natalie Grueninger on the subject of how Anne may have been expressing herself in her letters to Henry: Grueninger, Natalie and Sandra Vasoli. *All Things Boleyn with Sandra Vasoli, Episode 71*, Talking Tudors podcast, 1 May 2020.
https://talkingtudors.podbean.com/e/episode-71-all-things-boleyn-with-sandra-vasoli/

Grueninger, Natalie and James Peacock. *Boleyn Treasures with James Peacock, Episode 80*, Talking Tudors podcast, 27 June 2020. http://onthetudortrail.com/Blog/2020/06/27/episode-80-boleyn-treasures-with-james-peacock/

Henry & Anne: The Lovers Who Changed History. Directed by Chris Mitchell, performance by Professor Suzannah Lipscomb (self), Jack Hawkins & Emma Connell. Lion Television, 2014.

Digitized images of Anne's Book of Hours:
https://www.bl.uk/collection-items/anne-boleyn-book-of-hours

Henry VIII's letters in modern English:
https://www.theanneboleynfiles.com/resources/anne-boleyn-words/henry-viiis-love-letters-to-anne-boleyn/

"Claire Ridgway holds Anne Boleyn's Book of Hours at Hever Castle" Claire Ridgway vlog:
https://www.youtube.com/watch?v=XPeX2u8b6Sg&t=554s

Ship pendant:

Grueninger, Natalie and Sarah Morris. *Anne Boleyn's Coronation Procession with Sarah Morris, Episode 76*, Talking Tudors podcast, 30 May 2020
http://onthetudortrail.com/Blog/2020/05/30/episode-76-anne-boleyns-coronation-procession-with-sarah-morris/

The ship pendant from *The Tudors* appears to be from the Antiquities line of pendants within the *1928 brand of jewelry*. Currently, they have a similar one for sale. The item is: *ANTIQUITIES COUTURE SILVER-TONE BLACK ENAMEL CRYSTAL AND BLACK COSTUME PEARL GALLEON SHIP PIN Item # 38796 $140.00 USD.*

Courtship (continued):

There are three similar "vintage" (before 2000) *Antiquities* line ship pendants currently for sale on the Etsy shop "PalaceGallery" under the listing "Golden Realm Vintage Ship Brooch - Elizabethan Renaissance Victorian." Of course, I do not know how long supplies will last.

Additionally, in an Interview with *Showtime* Fan, 7 April 2008, Joan Bergin, costume designer for *The Tudors*, said she felt she "struck gold with a company…whose style is inspired by Elizabethan and antique fashion … (It is) called *Sorrelli* (and) run by two sisters—which is what the name means in Italian…" www.sorrelli.com. In addition, she cites jewelry makers *Tipperary Crystal* and *Autore*: http://www.thetudorswiki.com/page/JEWELLERY+of+the+Tudors

The Moost Happi:

Rood screen definition: A screen (also referred to as a choir screen) typically of richly carved wood or stone, separating the nave (the public) from the chancel (altar area) of a church. Rood screens are found throughout western Europe and date chiefly from the 14th–16th centuries. (Oxford Languages)

For further details on the history and imagery of the Rood Screen at King's College Chapel in Cambridge: http://www.lucychurchill.com/KingsCollegeChapelChoirScreen.php

Additional Information:

In addition to restoring *The Moost Happi Portrait Medal*, sculptor Lucy Churchill has also published an academically accepted translation of the iconography carved on the Rood Screen at King's College Chapel in Cambridge, which was commissioned by Henry and Anne in the early 1530's. Churchill found among the visual puns and ciphers celebrating Henry and Anne's union and royal status, the screen contains a clear and menacing threat to those who opposed their will.

It contains a prominent and disturbing image of a disembodied head, screaming in agony which, curiously, was long believed to depict Anne, beheaded on the charge of adultery. However, Churchill delved into this inconsistent detail to discover the head, held aloft by long hair, actually represents Absalom, the hirsute son of the Biblical King David, who met with an agonising death after rebelling against his father.

Other carvings on the screen and depictions elsewhere show how Henry increasingly self-identified with King David, God's chosen ruler. Anyone who questioned Henry and Anne's right to rule over the newly established Church of England—or the Act of Supremacy which disinherited Henry's Catholic daughter Mary—were put to death (for example, Moore and Fischer). Contemporary viewers would have clearly understood this chilling message within the carved imagery.

Churchill feels Anne's influence is all over the screen; not just in message, but in style, referencing Sir Pevsner's observations. Pevsner was an art historian and more specifically an architectural historian, who stated the screen is "The most exquisite piece of Italian (Renaissance) decoration surviving in England." Ives also says it is "The earliest major timber construction in the country entirely in Renaissance style". The Renaissance style was at the time truly cutting edge, and Anne was certainly "on message."

Churchill surmises that the style of screen, said to be the work of Burgundian carvers, is most likely the result of Anne's early cultural education at some of the grandest courts of Europe. "We know that Anne learned early on the power of visual imagery, and that she kept a close eye on the craftwork she commissioned. It is highly likely that Anne would have instigated, devised and supervised the realisation of this hugely significant project."

Grueninger, Natalie and Lucy Churchill. *Talking Tudors with Lucy Churchill, Episode 29*, Talking Tudors podcast, 17 April 2019. http://onthetudortrail.com/Blog/2019/04/17/18638/ (though some quotes are from personal responses from sculptor Lucy Churchill, July 2020)

Henry and Anne's Calais Itinerary: https://www.theanneboleynfiles.com/timeline-of-henry-viii-and-anne-boleyns-trip-to-calais-october-1532/

Anne's pregnancies: https://onthetudortrail.com/Blog/anne-boleyn/guest-articles/the-pregnancies-of-anne-boleyn/

Secret Whitehall Wedding: https://blog.hrp.org.uk/curators/a-secret-tudor-wedding/

Coronation:

The term "queen consort:" A *queen consort* is the wife of a reigning king…In contrast, a queen regnant is a queen in her own right with all the powers of a monarch, who (usually) has become queen by inheriting the throne upon the death of the previous monarch. (Wikipedia)

Additional information:

From historian Professor Eric Ives's description of Anne's official badge, the falcon is observed nurturing the growth of both the York and Lancastrian roses, symbols of Henry VIII's parents. Henry's mother's rose (York, white) and his father's rose (Lancaster, red), together make up the Tudor rose with the inclusion of these images atop the Plantagenet's "Woodstock" stump serving to remind viewers of Henry's right to the throne. Their growth up from the stump represents Anne's already evident fertility—life bursting "forth from the apparent barrenness of the Tudor stock," as Ives continues to point out. The crown on the falcon is an "imperial" crown emphasizing Henry's power as emperor and well apart from papal authority. "Finally, the bird had a scepter not only as a routine symbol of regality but as a sign of authority given by God," Ives concludes, "And the falcon is clearly a transmutation of the white dove which descended on the virgin Mary at the annunciation of Christ. The entire tableau welcomed Anne as the source of a revived Tudor family, a mother sent by God, whose pregnancy was according to the will of God's spirit, and one on whose head the crown would soon be placed as a sign of divine grace and acceptance;" thereby visually legitimizing Anne's divine place before God and within the Tudor Dynasty.

Link discussing Anne's Coronation and regal implements and crown: http://under-these-restless-skies.blogspot.com/2013/06/june-1-1533-anne-boleyns-coronation-day.html

Grueninger, Natalie and Sarah Morris. *Anne Boleyn's Coronation Procession with Sarah Morris, Episode 76*, Talking Tudors podcast, 30 May 2020. http://onthetudortrail.com/Blog/2020/05/30/episode-76-anne-boleyns-coronation-procession-with-sarah-morris/

Grueninger, Natalie and Dr. Alice Hunt. *Anne Boleyn's Coronation with Dr. Alice Hunt, Episode 77*, Talking Tudors podcast, 1 June 2020. http://onthetudortrail.com/Blog/2020/06/01/episode-77-anne-boleyns-coronation-with-dr-alice-hunt/

James Peacock's vlog post: https://www.youtube.com/watch?v=NLCJvNZC4qY

Tower:

Anne's purported scaffold speech: "Good Christian people, I have not come here to preach a sermon; I have come here to die. For according to the law and by the law I am judged to die, and therefore I will speak nothing against it. I am come hither to accuse no man, nor to speak of that whereof I am accused and condemned to die, but I pray God save the King and send him long to reign over you, for a gentler nor a more merciful prince was there never, and to me he was ever a good, a gentle, and sovereign lord. **And if any person will meddle of my cause, I require them to judge the best.** And thus I take my leave of the world and of you all, and I heartily desire you all to pray for me." ~ from *History Extra: The Final Days of Anne Boleyn: Why Did She Die?* Historyextra.com

Grueninger, Natalie and Dr. Lauren MacKay. *Boleyn Supporters at Court with Dr. Lauren MacKay, Episode 75*, Talking Tudors podcast, 26 May 2020. http://onthetudortrail.com/Blog/2020/05/26/episode-75-boleyn-supporters-at-court-with-dr-lauren-mackay/

Grueninger, Natalie and Beth von Staats. *Thomas Cranmer and the Boleyns with Beth von Staats, Episode 9*, Talking Tudors podcast, 20 June 2020. http://onthetudortrail.com/Blog/2020/06/20/episode-79-thomas-cranmer-the-boleyns-with-beth-von-staats/

Tower (continued):

Dress and Crown: For her research and imagination, I greatly appreciate the work of Joan Bergin, costume designer for "The Tudors" series. I feel she communicates much of the narrative through her designs. She did so again, here, in the scenes of Anne's arrest, which inspired the dress and crown on this page. An article about her work can be found here: http://fashion.telegraph.co.uk/news-features/TMG8416732/Henry-VIII-dressed-to-kill.html.

Interview about the clothing and jewelry in "The Tudors" with Joan Bergin: https://www.youtube.com/watch?v=MhO0SQYBTd0

Interview with Joan Bergin in the New York Times: https://archive.nytimes.com/www.nytimes.com/2009/06/07/arts/television/07berg.html

Interview with Joan Bergin by Stage and Screen Design Ireland: http://stageandscreendesignireland.ie/designers/joan-bergin/

Finally, I apologize to British readers: Although the spelling of certain words have remained within the British standard, American punctuation has been used (as it is what I am used to…) but when it comes to other things, I am sure there is much good which could be emulated from your country—a place I was unable to return to, as planned, in the Spring of 2020. The work on this book was my journey, for now.

> *"Chapuys saying she was braver than a lion; Cromwell saying she had intelligence, spirit and courage—that's incredible really . . . Whatever people's views on Anne Boleyn, no one can deny she had those things in abundance"*
>
> ~ James Peacock
>
> *Founder of "The Anne Boleyn Society"; queenanneboleyn.com; instagram: @Society_Anne*

Anne Boleyn's 'The Moost Happi' Portrait Medal

"Lucy Churchill's brilliant achievement has brought us as close to the real Anne Boleyn as we shall ever be able to get."
~ Professor Eric Ives, OBE

MAGNET
Dimensions: 38mm x 3mm (+2mm)
Material: Cold-cast bronze resin
Weight: 23g
Each medal is individually hand-cast in England
To buy: **AnneBoleynMoostHappi.Etsy.com**
Cost: £12 including postage & packing

PENDANT
Dimensions: 25mm x 1.5mm
Material: Available in a range of precious and semi-precious metals
Made to order by **Shapeways.com**
Cost: Price varies according to choice of metal and finish

WALL PLAQUE
Dimensions: 145mm x 7mm
Material: Cold-cast bronze resin
Weight: 250–300g
Each plaque is individually hand-cast in England
To buy: **AnneBoleynMoostHappi.Etsy.com**
Cost: £40, plus postage

For more information visit www.lucychurchill.com

Colouring History: Tudor Queens and Consorts

by Natalie Grueninger and Kathryn Holeman

"It had me hooked and before I knew it, two hours of relaxing colouring had passed—definitely a great escape on a Sunday afternoon! I also learned something along the way, as every image presented had a brief description to help set the scene. Learning and colouring, what's not to love?"
~ Sandra Alvarez, Editor of *The Medieval Magazine*

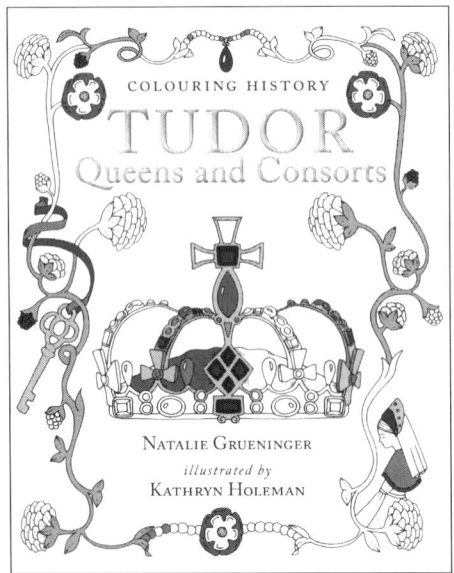

Delve into the dazzling—and dangerous—world of Tudor queens and consorts with this lavishly illustrated colouring book for grown-ups. Featuring an array of beautiful illustrations inspired by contemporary paintings and manuscripts, this keepsake book is sure to delight even the most discerning Tudor history buff and colouring aficionado.

8in x 10in paperback, 96 pages with 45 single-sided full page illustrations and historical reference captions. You will find this book and other Tudor gifts at **ColouringTudorHistory.com** or **KathrynHoleman.Etsy.com**